RELIGIONS AROUND THE WORLD

Catholicism

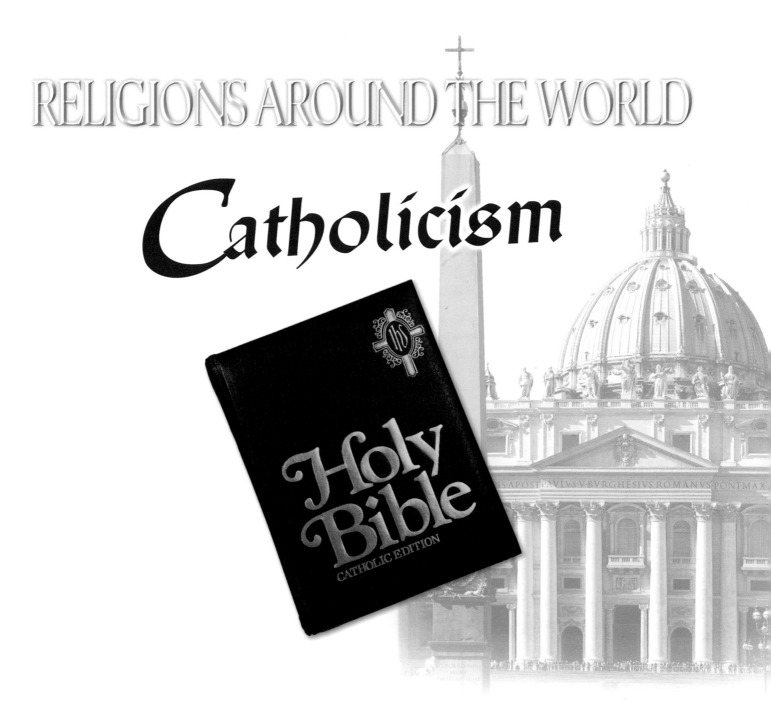

Katy Gerner

Marshall Cavendish
Benchmark
New York

This edition first published in 2009 in the United States of America by Marshall Cavendish Benchmark.

Marshall Cavendish Benchmark
99 White Plains Road
Tarrytown, NY 10591
www.marshallcavendish.us

All Internet sites were available and accurate when sent to press.

First published in 2008 by
MACMILLAN EDUCATION AUSTRALIA PTY LTD
15–19 Claremont Street, South Yarra 3141

Visit our website at www.macmillan.com.au or go directly to www.macmillanlibrary.com.au

Associated companies and representatives throughout the world.

Copyright © Katy Gerner 2008

Library of Congress Cataloging-in-Publication Data

Gerner, Katy.
    Catholicism / by Katy Gerner.
        p. cm. — (Religions around the world)
    Includes index.
    ISBN 978-0-7614-3165-7
    1. Catholic Church. I. Title.
    BX1754.G385 2008
282—dc22

                    2008002842

Edited by Erin Richards
Text and cover design by Cristina Neri, Canary Graphic Design
Photo research by Legend Images
Illustration on p. 14 by Andy Craig and Nives Porcellato
Map courtesy of Geo Atlas; modified by Raul Diche

Printed in the United States

Acknowledgments

The author would like to thank Father Con Campbell, Julie Daly and Glenn Martin for their suggestions, their wisdom and their time spent reviewing this book.

The author and the publisher are grateful to the following for permission to reproduce copyright material:

Front cover photograph (main): A family prays at an Ash Wednesday Mass, New York, 2007 courtesy of AAP Image/AP Photo/Kathy Willens. Other images: book background © Felix Möckel/iStockphoto; bible © PhotoSpin, Inc/Alamy; Notre Dame Cathedral © Robert Hill/iStockphoto; St Peter's Basilica © Roberto A Sanchez/iStockphoto; stained-glass window © Jim DeLillo/iStockphoto; cross © Neil Sullivan/iStockphoto.

Photos courtesy of: © Thierry Sébaut/Fotolia, 22 (bottom); © Vim Woodenhands/Fotolia, 25 (top), 28 (bottom); Getty Images, 13 (top center); Luis Acosta/AFP/Getty Images, 16; Noah Seelam/AFP/Getty Images, 24; Noel Coypel/The Bridgeman Art Library/Getty Images, 6; Lucas Cranach the Elder/The Bridgeman Art Library/Getty Images, 12 (left); Cosimo Rosselli/The Bridgeman Art Library/ Getty Images, 9 (top); Photo by William Thomas Cain/Getty Images, 19 (right); Hank Walker/Time & Life Pictures/Getty Images, 18 (left); © Gunther Beck/iStockphoto, 27 (top); © Aman Khan/iStockphoto, 4 (bottom center left); © Vasko Miokovic/iStockphoto, 4 (center); © Owusu-Ansah/iStockphoto, 4 (bottom center right); © Roberto A Sanchez/iStockphoto, 5 (top); © Sal Sen/iStockphoto, 26; © Richard Stamper/iStockphoto, 4 (bottom right); © Bob Thomas/iStockphoto, 4 (bottom left), 30 (top center); © Richard Vdovjak/iStockphoto, 21 (left); NASA Goddard Space Flight Center, 4 (center behind); © The Print Collector/Alamy/Photolibrary, 11 (bottom); Photos.com, 29; © PhotoSpin, Inc/Alamy, 1 (left), 10 (top); © Youssef Fraiwat/PhotoStockPlus, 7; © Zygimantas Cepaitis/ Shutterstock, 17 (left); © Alexander Kalina/Shutterstock, 20 (top left); © Paul Maguire/Shutterstock, 15 (left), 32; © José Correia Marafona/Shutterstock, 21 (right); © Martine Oger/Shutterstock, 5 (bottom); © Morozova Oksana/Shutterstock, 8; © Buturlimov Paul/ Shutterstock, 23; © photobank.ch/Shutterstock, 20 (bottom); © Gordon Swanson/Shutterstock, 4 (top).

Photos used in book design: book background © Felix Möckel/iStockphoto, 9, 10, 11, 15; cross © Neil Sullivan/iStockphoto, 3, 15; cross © Duncan Walker/iStockphoto, 17, 30; Notre Dame Cathedral © Robert Hill/iStockphoto, 3, 13; parchment background © Andrey Zyk/iStockphoto, 12, 13, 18, 19; Rosary beads © Paul Maguire/Shutterstock, 3; St Peter's Basilica © Roberto A Sanchez/ iStockphoto, 1, 7, 9, 15, 20, 21, 22, 27, 28, 30; stone tablets based on image by james steidl/iStockphoto, 10.

While every care has been taken to trace and acknowledge copyright, the publisher tenders their apologies for any accidental infringement where copyright has proved untraceable. Where the attempt has been unsuccessful, the publisher welcomes information that would redress the situation.

For Sarah, Steve, Emilie and Benjamin

1 3 5 6 4 2

Contents

Glossary words

When a word is printed in **bold**, you can look up its meaning in the Glossary on page 31.

World Religions

Religion is a belief in a supernatural power that must be loved, worshipped, and obeyed. A world religion is a religion that is practiced throughout the world. The five core world religions are Christianity, Islam, Hinduism, Buddhism and Judaism.

People practicing a religion follow practices that they believe are pleasing to their god or gods. Followers read sacred **scriptures** and may worship either privately at home or in a place of worship. They often carry out special rituals, such as when a baby is born, a couple gets married, or someone dies. Religious people have beliefs about how they should behave in this life, and also about life after death.

Learning about world religions can help us to understand each other's differences. We learn about the different ways people try to lead good lives and make the world a better place.

World religions are practiced by many people of different cultures.

Catholicism

Catholicism is the oldest Christian **denomination**. The three main branches of Christianity are Catholicism, the Orthodox Church, and Protestantism. The denominations all have slightly different ways of practicing their religions, such as:

✠ the ways they worship

✠ who they allow to be church leaders

✠ how they solve certain problems.

Catholics, like all Christians, believe there are three persons in one God:

✠ the Father

✠ the Son, Jesus Christ

✠ the Holy Spirit.

They believe Jesus came to Earth to teach people to love God and one another.

The head of the Catholic Church is the Pope, who runs the Church from **Vatican City** in Rome, in Italy. Only men can be appointed to the role of Pope. The leadership roles of cardinals, archbishops, bishops, and priests are also taken by men. Women can become religious sisters, or nuns, and work for the church community or join an **enclosed order**.

Many Catholic churches are very beautiful buildings. Some of the world's most beautiful architecture and decoration can be found in the cathedrals and churches of Europe. These buildings often have statues, stained-glass windows, ornate furniture, and paintings on the walls.

Saint Peter's Basilica in Vatican City in Rome, Italy.

Many Catholic churches and cathedrals are very ornate.

Religious Beliefs

This painting shows the resurrection of Jesus.

Catholics believe that God listens to their prayers and that **saints** can pray for them. They believe in the **Holy Trinity** and that they must serve God in whatever role he chooses for them.

Answered Prayers

Catholics believe that they can pray to God and that he will answer their prayers. They also believe that they can ask saints to pray to God with them. Catholics may ask Saint Christopher, the **patron saint** of travelers, to pray for them before they go on a journey. Or they may ask Saint Thomas Aquinas, patron saint of students, to pray for them before an exam.

The Holy Trinity

The Holy Trinity is made up of:

✠ God, the Father, who made heaven and Earth

✠ Jesus, the son of God, who came to Earth and is the **Messiah**

✠ The Holy Spirit, who guides and strengthens people.

Catholics believe that Jesus came to Earth and was born a Jew in Israel to a woman called Mary. Jesus was **crucified** by people who did not believe in him. He died, but was **resurrected** and went back to heaven to be with God. Catholics hope that when they die, they will also go to heaven.

Serving God

Catholics believe that one way to serve God is to become a priest or a religious sister or brother. This is a decision that is taken for life, and priests and religious sisters or brothers must not marry.

Priests are Christ's representatives and are usually in charge of a **parish**. They celebrate Mass and the **sacraments**, and deliver **sermons** to the **congregation**. Some priests work for, or run, Catholic organizations, such as the Caritas charitable organization and various Vatican departments.

Religious sisters usually live together and work in the community, as do religious brothers. The fields they work in include:

- ✠ education
- ✠ health
- ✠ welfare
- ✠ spiritual and personal development
- ✠ youth
- ✠ ministry to refugees
- ✠ ministry to victims of crime and to prisoners.

Priests in the Catholic Church are always male.

Beliefs About Behavior

Catholics have a number of beliefs about how they should behave. Catholics believe they should receive the sacraments, love their neighbor and follow Jesus' teachings.

Reconciliation often takes place in a confessional.

The Seven Sacraments

The seven sacraments are:

✠ Baptism. The priest pours water, in the sign of the cross, on the forehead of the person being baptized, usually a child, to welcome them into the church. Baptism is believed to cleanse the soul of **original sin**.

✠ Reconciliation. Catholics tell their sins to a priest and promise to try not to **sin** again. The priest then forgives them in God's name.

✠ Confirmation. A person becomes an adult member of the church and confirms the promises made for the person at the baptism.

✠ Holy Communion. This takes place during Mass. Catholics receive a wafer of bread and sometimes a sip of wine, which they believe have become the body and blood of Jesus.

✠ Marriage. A man and woman promise themselves to each other for life.

✠ Anointing of the sick. Holy oil is placed on the foreheads of the sick or dying.

✠ Ordination. The process of becoming a priest.

Catholics receive most of these sacraments, although only priests receive the sacrament of ordination.

This painting shows Jesus's Sermon on the Mount.

Loving Their Neighbor

Jesus told his **disciples** they should love their neighbor as much as they love themselves. This doesn't just mean being nice to the people next door. It means treating all people the way you would like to be treated, with kindness, love, and respect. Many Catholics help their neighbors by doing voluntary work for organizations, such as Saint Vincent de Paul, Caritas, and the Catholic Commission for Justice and Peace.

Sermon on the Mount

Jesus's most specific teaching about behavior was the Sermon on the Mount. Jesus preached while he was sitting on the side of a mountain near Lake Galilee. He taught many things about how he wanted people to behave.

FROM THE SERMON ON THE MOUNT

✠ Love your enemies and forgive them when they do bad things to you.

✠ Trust and depend on God and do not worry about what you are going to eat, drink, or wear.

✠ Do not judge other people.

9

Scriptures

Catholics believe that the Christian Bible is inspired by God. The Catholic Bible is made up of thirty-nine books in the Old Testament and twenty-seven books in the New Testament.

The Old Testament

The Old Testament contains law, history, poetry, and **prophecies**. It describes how the world was created, how Israel became a nation, and the work done by the kings and the prophets. It also includes the Ten Commandments, which tell people how they should live.

The Deuterocanonical Books

The Catholic Old Testament contains twelve more books than the Protestant Old Testament. These are called the Deuterocanonical books. They were written around 200 or 300 BCE and contain history, law, advice, and poetry.

Sirach is one of the books included in the Old Testament.

If you eat too much you'll get sick; if you do it all the time, you'll always have stomach trouble.

SIRACH 37:30

The Lord created medicines from the earth, and a sensible person will not hesitate to use them.

SIRACH 38:4

Catholics believe that the Bible is the word of God.

1 Do not worship any other gods and do not make any idols
2 Do not misuse the name of God
3 Keep the Sabbath holy
4 Honor your father and mother
5 Do not murder
6 Do not commit adultery
7 Do not steal
8 Do not lie
9 Do not covet your neighbor's wife
10 Do not covet your neighbor's goods

The Ten Commandments

The New Testament

The New Testament was first published in 150 CE, although the books were written much earlier. It has twenty-seven books, including:

✠ the four Gospels, written by Jesus's disciples Matthew, Mark, Luke, and John. They tell about the life and teachings of Jesus

✠ history

✠ prophecies

✠ letters, written mainly by Saint Paul, who was an important leader of the early church

✠ Acts, which tells how Jesus's followers, especially Saint Peter and Saint Paul, spread his teachings to different parts of the world.

Paul wrote many of his letters while he was imprisoned by the Romans for his beliefs.

Paul's Letters

Saint Paul traveled widely, teaching and setting up churches. He wrote many letters to the early Christians, explaining about Jesus, answering their questions and helping them with their problems. Saint Paul's letters are considered a very important part of the New Testament.

Saint Paul wrote a letter to Christians in the Greek city of Corinth around 57 CE.

> Love is patient and kind; it is not jealous or conceited or proud; love is not ill-mannered or selfish or irritable, love does not keep a record of wrongs; love is not happy with evil, but is happy with the truth. Love never gives up; and its faith, hope, and patience never fail.
>
> I CORINTHIANS 13:4–8

Religious Leaders

Two important leaders in the early Christian church were Saint Peter and Saint Paul. They are called saints because the Catholic Church has recognized the holiness of their lives.

Saint Peter   ?–62 CE

Peter was one of the first **apostles**. He was very headstrong, often doing and saying the wrong thing, but Jesus was very fond of him. Peter was originally a fisherman but left to follow Jesus.

Peter asked Jesus many questions to understand his teachings better. His conversations with Jesus are written in the New Testament so all Christians can learn from them. Peter was the first disciple to realize that Jesus was the Son of God.

When Jesus was arrested and taken away to be killed, Peter pretended he did not know him. This was because he was afraid of being arrested, too. After Jesus's resurrection, Peter became very brave and traveled to many different cities around Israel, preaching about Jesus.

Peter was crucified upside down in 62 CE during a Christian **persecution**. Catholics believe Peter asked to be crucified in this way because he did not consider himself worthy of the same death as Jesus.

Saint Peter is often shown holding a key because Jesus gave Peter the "Keys to the Kingdom of Heaven."

Saint Paul preached about Jesus and established many new churches.

Saint Paul
around 10—around 62 CE

Paul was originally called Saul of Tarsus. Paul did not approve of Christians. He was on his way to arrest some when he heard Jesus, whom he believed was dead, speaking to him. This changed his life. He became a Christian and one of the most important leaders in the early church.

At the time Paul became a Christian, non-Jewish Christians were expected to observe all the Jewish rituals and food laws.

Paul introduced the idea of a universal church that non-Jews could belong to without having to obey all these laws.

Paul traveled widely, preaching about Jesus and establishing churches. He organized money for poor people and wrote many letters, which are included in the New Testament.

Paul was eventually beheaded during a time when Christians were being persecuted. He is called an apostle, even though he did not meet Jesus during his time on Earth. Paul heard Jesus speaking to him after Jesus had returned to heaven.

Worship Practices

All Christians share similar worship practices, such as prayers, Bible readings, and Holy Communion. The Catholic Church has the sacrament of reconciliation which is not practised by the Protestant Church. Another practice followed by Catholics but not Protestants is praying the rosary.

Reconciliation

Reconciliation, which used to be called penance or "going to confession," is a time for Catholics to seek forgiveness for their sins. Catholics can discuss with their priest how to improve their behavior and ask to **receive absolution**. Reconciliation is often held in a reconciliation room. The person confessing sits opposite the priest and confesses his or her sins. The person then says that he or she is sorry and wants to change for the better. They then pray together and the priest forgives the person on behalf of Jesus. The priest may also ask the person to recite some prayers as **penance**.

Catholics are expected to go to reconciliation at least once a year. Some Catholics prefer not to see the priest when they confess their sins. Instead, they speak to the priest from behind a screen.

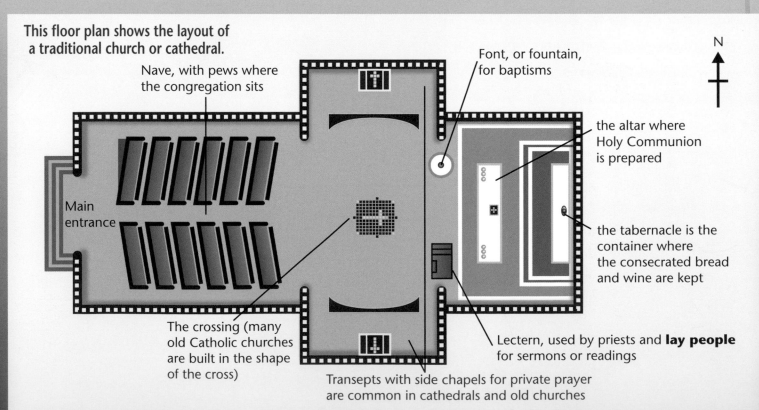

This floor plan shows the layout of a traditional church or cathedral.

N

Nave, with pews where the congregation sits

Font, or fountain, for baptisms

the altar where Holy Communion is prepared

Main entrance

the tabernacle is the container where the consecrated bread and wine are kept

The crossing (many old Catholic churches are built in the shape of the cross)

Lectern, used by priests and **lay people** for sermons or readings

Transepts with side chapels for private prayer are common in cathedrals and old churches

Rosary Beads

Catholics use rosary beads to help them recite the rosary, which is a structured prayer to Mary, the Mother of Jesus. The rosary is made up of introductory prayers, five decades of the rosary, and concluding prayers. A decade of the rosary is one *Our Father*, ten *Hail Marys*, and one *Glory Be to the Father*.

Rosary beads help Catholics to count the three *Hail Marys* in the introductory prayers and the ten *Hail Marys* in the decades. The beads have a crucifix, a single bead, then three beads together, and another bead attached to a holy medal. Attached to the medal is a chain with five groups of ten beads, separated from each other by another bead.

Rosary beads are an aid to help Catholics recite the rosary.

OUR FATHER

Our Father, who art in Heaven,
hallowed be thy name.
Thy kingdom come,
thy will be done
on Earth as it is in Heaven.
Give us this day our daily bread
and forgive us our trespasses,
as we forgive those who trespass against us.
And lead us not into temptation,
but deliver us from evil. Amen.

HAIL MARY

Hail Mary, full of grace,
The Lord is with thee.
Blessed art thou among women,
and blessed is the fruit of thy womb, Jesus.
Holy Mary, Mother of God,
pray for us sinners,
now and at the hour of our death. Amen.

GLORY BE TO THE FATHER

Glory be to the Father, and to the Son, and to the Holy Spirit.
As it was in the beginning, is now and ever shall be, world
without end. Amen.

A Mexican woman being marked
with ash to commemorate
Ash Wednesday

Festivals and Celebrations

Religious seasons that are very important to Catholics are Lent,
Advent, and Christmas.

Lent

The season of Lent lasts for forty days. It is the spiritual preparation for Easter,
which is when Christians remember the crucifixion and resurrection of Jesus.
Lent begins on Ash Wednesday, when some Catholics go to a special Mass.
During the service, the priest puts a cross of ashes on the forehead of each
worshipper. The ashes symbolize that the worshippers are sorry for their sins.

Good Deeds

Catholics believe they should do good things during Lent, things that will help
them become better people. Some things Catholics might do during Lent include:

✠ helping people worse off than themselves

✠ doing kind deeds without expecting thanks

✠ going to Mass during the week, not just on Sundays

✠ praying

✠ meditating

✠ doing the Stations of the Cross, which is a meditation on how Jesus suffered
when he was crucified.

At Christmastime, Nativity scenes can be found in many Catholic churches.

Advent and Christmas

Advent is celebrated for four weeks before Christmas, which is when Christians celebrate the birth of Jesus. Advent is a time to prepare spiritually for Christmas. Catholics practice many traditions during Advent and Christmas.

Candles

During Advent, four candles are put up in the church and surrounded by a wreath, which represents eternity. One candle is lit each Sunday. On Christmas Eve a fifth candle, called a "Christ Candle," is placed in the center of the wreath. The Christ Candle is then lit to celebrate Jesus's birth. Special hymns are sung and Bible passages read during this time.

The Nativity

Some Catholic communities put on a Nativity play, in which children act out the birth of Jesus. Others have a Nativity scene in the church, which shows baby Jesus with his parents, surrounded by the people, animals, and angels who came to worship him.

Gifts and Cards

Catholics often give and receive presents at Christmas. They also buy presents for poor people, give money to charity, and send Christmas cards to friends and family.

There are many holy days and festivals throughout the year that are important to Catholics. Here are some of them:

Lent
For the forty days before Easter
February, March or April

St Patrick's Day
March 17

Holy Week
The week that ends in Easter Sunday
Late March or April

Assumption of Mary
August 15

All Saints Day
November 1

Advent
For the four weeks before Christmas
Late November and December

Immaculate Conception of Mary
December 8

Christmas Day
December 25

Important Catholics

Two important Catholics who brought about change in the Catholic Church were Pope John XXIII and Saint Katherine Drexel.

Pope John XXIII   1881-1963

Pope John XXIII was ordained as a priest in 1904. During World War II he helped the **Jewish underground** and saved thousands of refugees in Europe. He was elected Pope in 1958, aged 76.

In 1962, Pope John XXIII called a major meeting of the bishops of the world, called the Second Vatican Council. The council discussed how the Church could bring a new understanding of its teachings to the people.

This began many changes within the Catholic Church:

✠ Mass could be said in the local language of a church, instead of only in Latin

✠ followers were encouraged to read the Bible for themselves, instead of only hearing it read in church

✠ priests, sisters, and brothers could wear more modern and comfortable clothing instead of the traditional robes and habits

✠ Catholics could enter churches of other denominations

✠ lay people were encouraged to have a bigger role in church

Pope John XXIII is still known today as "Good Pope John." He was **beatified** in 2000 and may one day be declared a saint.

Pope John XXIII helped to reshape the Catholic Church.

Saint Katherine Drexel   1858–1955

Saint Katherine Drexel was born to a wealthy family in Philadelphia who taught her that wealth must be shared with everyone. When she received her inheritance, she decided to spend the money on American Indians and African Americans, and set up a number of organizations to help them.

She asked Pope Leo XIII to recommend a religious congregation to work in her organizations, but instead he recommended that she become a missionary herself. In 1889 she began her training in religious life with the Sisters of Mercy at Pittsburgh.

In 1891, Mother Katherine founded the Sisters of the Blessed Sacrament for Indians and Colored People. She was responsible for the opening of approximately sixty schools, forty mission centers, and Xavier University, New Orleans, which was the first university for African-American people in the United States. She was regularly harassed because of her work.

Mother Katherine was declared **venerable** in 1987, was beatified in 1988, and was **canonized** in October 2000. She died at the age of 96 at Cornwell Heights, Pennsylvania.

Saint Katherine Drexel was declared a saint in October 2000.

Birth

When babies are born into Catholic families, they are welcomed into the Church by baptism. They are also given a name, either from the New Testament or after a saint.

Baptism

The Baptism ceremony is almost always held in a church. Exceptions include if the baby is very sick in a hospital or, for cultural reasons, the parents want to perform the ceremony in an area sacred to them. During the Baptism ceremony:

✠ the parents promise to raise the child as a Catholic

✠ the godparents, one of whom must be a Catholic, promise to help the child be Catholic if the parents are unable to

✠ the priest pours water on the baby's head or the baby is dipped in water

✠ the priest makes the sign of the cross on the baby's head with holy oil.

After the baptism, there is often a party at the parents' home, and the family receives gifts for the baby.

The priest pours holy water over the baby's head during Baptism.

Choosing a Name

Catholic parents are encouraged to give their babies a name from the New Testament or to name the child after a saint. This custom goes back to around 33 CE. Catholics follow this custom for two reasons:

✠ it helps link the child to the Catholic community

✠ it encourages the child to learn more about the saint the child was named for and perhaps to take on the saint's qualities.

Popular Catholic names include:

✠ Christopher, which means "Christ bearer." Saint Christopher is the patron saint of travelers

✠ Michael, which means "like God." Michael was an important angel, or archangel

✠ John, which means "God has mercy." There were a number of Johns in the New Testament, including John the Baptist and John the disciple

✠ Mary, which means "beautiful." Mary was the Mother of Jesus and there were also two Marys who were followers of Jesus

✠ Anne, which means "grace." Anne was the mother of Mary and grandmother of Jesus

✠ Catherine, which means "pure." There are several Saint Catherines.

Saint Michael the Archangel is the patron saint of soldiers and police officers.

Growing Up

Two important sacraments for Catholic children growing up are Holy Communion and confirmation.

Holy Communion

When children are about eight years old, or sometimes older, they attend classes to prepare for the sacrament of Holy Communion. Holy Communion, which includes the celebration of the Eucharist, is a very old tradition. It goes back to the Last Supper, which is the meal Jesus had with his apostles before he was killed. At the meal, Jesus blessed the bread and wine and said, "This is my body and this is my blood. Do this in memory of me."

At Holy Communion, members of the congregation each receive a round wafer of bread and sometimes a sip of wine. Catholics believe the blessed bread and wine become the body and blood of Jesus. The first Holy Communion is a very special occasion and children wear beautiful clothes on the day. They may also receive a certificate from the priest and presents from their friends and relatives. The presents may include rosary beads, plaques, crosses, Bibles, and prayer books.

Catholic girls often wear white dresses to their first Holy Communion, and boys may wear white suits.

Confirmation

Confirmation is also a very special day for Catholic children. Confirmation is to remind Catholics that the Holy Spirit came to the disciples after Jesus had risen from the dead and gone back to heaven. Children must have received the sacrament of Reconciliation, and attend classes to study the Catholic faith before being confirmed.

Confirmation ceremonies are held in a church. The children must choose to keep their baptismal saint's name or choose another saint's name to add to their name. The bishop calls the children by this name, places his hand on their heads, and draws a cross on the children's foreheads with holy oil.

The children may also receive a certificate from the bishop and presents, such as rosary beads, crosses, and prayer books, from friends and relatives.

Marriage

A Catholic wedding is a sacrament and a legally binding occasion.

Preparing for Marriage

There is much preparation before a Catholic wedding. The couple must be certain that they love each other and can cope with married life. Engaged couples must attend marriage preparation classes and attend talks with their priest.

Beliefs about Marriage

Catholics have a number of beliefs about marriage, including:

✠ that getting married is a sacrament and a vocation

✠ that marriage symbolizes the relationship between Jesus and the Church

✠ that a marriage should last for life

✠ that being married teaches a couple more about God's love

✠ that a person should not have sex before marriage and can only have sex with the person they marry.

Divorce

The Catholic Church does not believe in divorce but will annul, or make void, a marriage under certain conditions. Grounds for annulment include:

✠ if either party was forced into the marriage

✠ if either party was too young or did not understand what marriage is all about

✠ if either party is unable to carry out the duties of marriage

✠ if either party does not intend to have children

The bride's white wedding dress represents purity.

Wedding Ceremony

A Catholic wedding ceremony is almost always held in a Catholic church. This is because it is a sacrament.

During the ceremony, the priest preaches about marriage and leads the congregation in prayer, and special hymns are sung. In front of the priest and the congregation, the couple promise that they will always love, respect, and be faithful to each other, through good times and bad times. They give each other rings to wear, which symbolize the unbroken bonds of marriage. A single candle is lit to symbolize that the two people are now joined together as one. Finally, the couple and two witnesses sign the wedding register and the priest officially introduces the married couple to the congregation.

Exchanging wedding rings is an important part of a Catholic wedding ceremony.

Death and the Afterlife

Catholics have important customs that they practice just before and after a person dies. They also believe there is an afterlife.

The Last Rites

When Catholics are dying, they receive the last rites from a priest. This is called anointing the sick, and is a sacrament given to both the sick and the dying. The priest anoints the person's forehead with holy oil. He prays that the person will be made better or that if the person dies, that they will go to heaven to be with Jesus. The priest will also give absolution for their sins.

A priest reads a prayer at the cemetery before the coffin is buried.

The Funeral

Catholic funerals are usually held within a week of the person dying. There is a church service with prayers, hymns, and Scripture readings, and the priest blesses the coffin with holy water.

After the service, the coffin is taken to the cemetery, where more prayers are said to send the person's soul to Jesus. Traditionally, Catholics were always buried rather than **cremated**. Today, the Church recommends burial but does not forbid cremation.

A wake may be held at the funeral home or family home before a funeral. Wakes can go for a few hours or longer. During this time, family and friends gather to pray for the person and remember them, and to comfort each other.

This painting shows heaven on the left, Jesus in the middle and hell on the right.

60 A. FRA ANGELICO (1400-1455) DAS JÜNGSTE GERICHT

Life After Death

Catholics believe that after they die, they will be judged by God according to how they lived on Earth. This judgment will determine if they are sent to heaven to be with Jesus, to purgatory, or to hell.

Catholics believe:

✠ Heaven is a wonderful place where there is no fighting, no sadness, no pain, no hatred, and it is always peaceful. It is a spiritual home where you live with God, Jesus, the prophets, and the angels forever.

✠ Purgatory is a place where souls are cleansed and prepared for life in heaven. Not everyone needs to go through purgatory. People who have lived good, holy lives go straight to heaven, as do those who suffered a "purgatory" in life because of illness, poverty, or persecution.

✠ Hell is a lonely, terrible place where souls are separated from God forever. People who go there do not care about God, anyone, or anything. There are also demons in hell. They were once angels but they disobeyed God. The main demon is Lucifer. People who go to hell are doomed to be there forever. No prayer will help them.

Catholicism Around the World

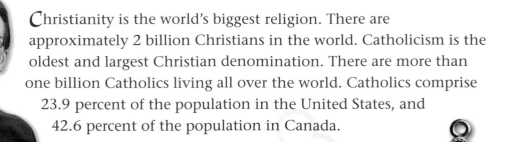

Christianity is the world's biggest religion. There are approximately 2 billion Christians in the world. Catholicism is the oldest and largest Christian denomination. There are more than one billion Catholics living all over the world. Catholics comprise 23.9 percent of the population in the United States, and 42.6 percent of the population in Canada.

This map shows the top ten Catholic countries.

ARCTIC OCEAN

ARCTIC OCEAN

SPAIN
94 percent

SAN MARINO
100 percent

VATICAN CITY
100 percent

DOMINICAN REPUBLIC
95 percent

MALTA
98 percent

ATLANTIC OCEAN

PACIFIC OCEAN

HONDURAS
97 percent

VENEZUELA
96 percent

EAST TIMOR
98 percent

PACIFIC OCEAN

ECUADOR
95 percent

INDIAN OCEAN

BOLIVIA
95 percent

N
W — E
S

KEY

■	area of country
SPAIN	name of country
94 percent	percentage of country population that is Catholic

SOUTHERN OCEAN

SOUTHERN OCEAN

Glossary

apostles	the disciples Jesus chose to work in his ministry, Saint Paul, and the Gospel writers
beatified	blessed by the Pope, and the step before becoming a saint
canonized	made a saint
congregation	a group of people meeting to worship God
cremated	burning a dead body until only ashes are left
crucified	nailed to a wooden cross
denomination	a branch of Christianity, such as Catholic or Anglican
disciples	followers of Jesus
enclosed order	a religious order where monks or nuns must stay in their monastery or convent
excommunicated	expelled from the Catholic Church and not allowed to receive the sacraments
fasting	not eating, or eating very little
habit	clothes that a religious sister, or nun, wears
Holy Trinity	God in three persons: the Father, the Son, and the Holy Spirit
Jewish underground	a movement that tried to save Jews from being captured by the Nazis during World War II
lay people	Catholics who are not priests or religious brothers or sisters
Messiah	in Christianity, the savior of all Christians, Jesus Christ
original sin	the first sin, committed by Adam and Eve when they ate the forbidden fruit in the Garden of Eden, which is said to mark all human souls
parish	an area that includes at least one church, over which a priest presides
patron saint	a saint who is considered to be a defender of a person, group, or nation
penance	an action to show that you are sorry for your behavior
persecution	the poor treatment of people because of their religious beliefs
prophecies	knowledge about the future, said to be obtained from God
receive absolution	to have your sins forgiven by a priest (acting on behalf of Jesus)
resurrected	brought back to life
sacraments	special religious ceremonies
saints	people whose holy lives have been recognized by the Catholic Church
scriptures	sacred writings
sermons	speeches that teach about sections of the Bible or other scriptures
sin	to commit bad actions
Vatican City	the capital of the Catholic Church where the Pope lives in Rome, Italy
venerable	the first step in becoming a saint

Index